Unsaid

OrangeBooks Publication

1st Floor, Rajhans Arcade, Mall Road, Kohka, Bhilai, Chhattisgarh - 490020

Website:**www.orangebooks.in**

© Copyright, 2024, Author

All rights reserved. No part of this book may be reproduced, stored in a retrieval system, or transmitted, in any form by any means, electronic, mechanical, magnetic, optical, chemical, manual, photocopying, recording or otherwise, without the prior written consent of its writer.

First Edition, 2024

"People and memories that became words"

These were written over 10 years period...

"Camper"

docile, yet alert,
aware of my desires.
acknowledging the brewing thunderstorm,
stubborn as i am.
hopelessly romantic,
believing in magic and monsters.
forewarned against entry,
"only to be shattered."
yet, i've pitched my tent in the storm,
now adrift,
chasing the wind...

"Smokers dilemma"

people come and go,
yet here you stand alone.
what is your dream ?
waiting for inspiration to ignite,
what is it you truly seek ?
wasting life in smoke,
are we just awaiting our demise ?
i fail to comprehend,
feeling threatened by the unknown.
longing to dwell in the present,
to shun thoughts of tomorrow.
for the future appears daunting...

"Tear drop"

heart heavy,
congestion in his chest.
memories in his eyes,
falling as droplets.
all he offered was love,
all he received was hurt.
sitting in darkness,
awaiting release.
the congestion fades,
but memories linger on.
head heavy,
hands shaky.
he emerges from the room,
feeling renewed, invigorated.
yet she returns,
placing him back in his former anguish.
now weakened,
unable to ignore or forget,
the freshness fades away.

"Same old story"

heart desires her,
mind advises to steer clear.
repeated warnings,
yet repeats the same error.
deaf to advice,
indifferent to the present.
simply going with the flow.
sometimes ponders,
"what if?"
the flow leads astray.
attempts to seize control,
chaos ensues.
plunging from a waterfall,
no true mastery.
paranoia instructs,
all one can do is,
just go with the flow.

"Always think about yourself first"

people dying, people crying,
trying to feel, their feel
blank expression on my face
imagining their pain
imagine their faces
busy in our own world
some people care
some people show
how are we to help
praying is the not the answer
helping them is not enough
only time can heal them
bring back their laughter.
sitting on the rubble
wondering when it's going to end,
maybe in few years
it's going to flourish again.

"Wave surfer"

it arrives like a wave in your mind,
a wave that slows down time.
you pause for a moment,
and everything seems to decelerate.
you feel as if someone is suffocating you,
your head grows cold,
and you're powerless to stop it,
it steals everything away.
you take deep breathe,
hoping, it will end.
but, it doesn't and,
deep inside you are calling out for help,
but outside you are calm as a cow.
it's coming to an end,
but it doesn't change anything.
the scar still remains,
and you try not to think about it
but you keep doing it.
head hurts, heart bleeds.

"It's a boat right"

a heart is akin to a boat,
if someone shatters it, the vessel sinks,
and the person aboard with it,
drowning into oblivion,
never to return from the depths of death.
often, it's a cystal boat,
resilient enough to withstand some blows,
but with each relentless strike,
and that final, fatal blow,
the boat succumbs, sinking into the abyss.
when it's plunging,
there's naught to be done but seek another vessel,
ensuring it's crafted from stone,
so it may withstand the onslaught,
and never break again.

"Conflict"

driving in a highway
she's sitting beside me
smoking a cigarette,
when she looked at me
moment became infinite.
anything was possible, but
bounded by our present
tormented by our past
just making that eye contact
i shy away.
scared, something will happen
connection was strong
completely honest to her,
shes going away,
stuck in a conflict
but that moment was infinite
and the feeling cant be explained.

"The waiting game"

tearing myself apart,
one pure soul corrupted by smoke.
anxiety in mind,
helplessness in body,
conflicting thoughts collide.
falling into the abyss
like a waterfall,
into nothingness and darkness.
overlooking nature,
seeing past it,
waiting for my miracle,
a potion of rejuvenation.

"Can you increase the saturation?"

returned to my reality,
hoping for brightness once more.
left everything, everyone behind,
believing it would improve.
reconciled with my past,
but now i see,
she's on the warpath,
slaying me from within.
losing myself a new,
words keeping me bound,
on the journey to reclaim my precious.
i pray it's not too late.

"Ground zero"

hollow body,
bed vibrating,
heart echoing,
mind soulless.
bloodshot eyes,
nose runny,
bones broken,
faith shattered.
euphoric state,
clock ticking,
time passing,
moving on.

"Free bird"

set yourself free,
release the bird,
shatter illusions,
embrace the truth.
a man without conscience is no man,
confront your deeds,
act upon them,
liberate yourself.
don't believe in god,
but in nature.
release the bird,
embrace the truth.

"Road to happiness"

i wish
this car,
could take me somewhere far.
where everyone is happy,
free from money,
just living their life,
without any worry.
i wish
for heaven,
where i can be with her,
without anyone holding me back,
just living our life.
in this world,
nothing is free
even happiness comes with a price.
i wish
to be buried,
so i won't be worried..

"Desolated"

here i am again,
mending the broken,
fleeing from the future,
remaining numb.
words have lost their power,
crumbling apart,
in the sands of time.
devoid of communication,
signs of intoxication,
engulfed in despair,
slowly withering
from within.

"Love in a park"

the kind of love
it's never gloomy,
walking hand in hand
through the amusement park
the kind of love
you eagerly await her arrival,
and when she's there,
your world bursts with color.
despite endless fights,
a single "i love you"
melts all the walls away.
the kind of love
where you refuse to let go,
fighting against all odds to stay together.
this kind of love,
this kind of love,
is hard to come by.

"Seeker"

in the midst of the sky,
i stand on a tall tower,
with my flesh and bone,
like a red pearl in the sky.
shining through the clouds,
it comes and goes,
but once it's seen,
the timeless beauty is captured by the eyes.
there are days black and white,
we are what we dream.
i will go on, till i shan't see the light.

"Stranger danger"

mystery in my heart,
confusion in my soul,
in a strange place,
where everyone is nice.
heart wanders on,
seeking a stranger,
though i know it's danger.
the land of sin,
where no one is kin,
you sow what you reap,
living forever.

"80s Dream"

once upon a time,
talking to a girl was a big deal,
but now a days...
once upon a time,
going on a date was a special occasion,
but now, not so much.
once upon a time,
girls were exclusive to one,
but now, it's different.
once upon a time...

"Daedalus was right"

a feeling,
heavy as a block,
lodged in the heart,
yearning for release.
scared of what may emerge,
yet compelled to unburden,
sitting with it,
but not for too long.
soar high,
forgetting the ground below,
only to fall.
rebuild,
protect my soul, won't you ?
i will return,
to soar once more.

"Looped"

construction and destruction
aspire inspire
learn and unlearn
where does it end ?
today blends into tomorrow,
night transitions to day,
fire fuels desire
are they all the same ?

"Brand new season"

the light hum of wind,
chirping and cawing,
footsteps echoing,
in the golden hour.
above the blue sky,
gazing straight,
flapping and flapping,
wind brushes my skin.
autumn is here,
just like that,
the season has changed.

"In the end, it's not upto me, what goes around comes back around"

tears of innocence,
scorching the floor,
rendering him numb,
transforming him into a devil.
seated in a chamber,
enveloped by molten lava,
a faint silhouette lingers,
filling him with remorse for his choices.
spirits stand by him,
avenging his tears,
echoes of the past,
avenging old sorrows,
for the decisions made long ago.
the cycle commences,
spirits set forth,
the world revolves,
in accordance with his desires now.
it cannot be halted.

"The wolf with the choice"

stuck in the tunnel,
darkness pervades,
hazy memories and nightmares.
as i walk forward,
two wolves stand guard,
black and white, their colors,
focus illuminates their forms.
which will lead me out ?

"Sinners and saints"

take my wings,
clip them,
for i am the fallen one.
let your wrath
descend upon me,
for i am the one.
but do not forget,
you and i,
are the same,
sinners and saints.
learning to fly,
once again.

"Facade"

is it an act,
or is it real ?
pretend to numb the pain,
too numb to even act.
for how long
will this continue ?
continue
until you die.

"Infinite dilemma"

surrender,
are you alive,
are you dead,
do you exist ?
influence,
die,
chemical will,
die already,
bury me,
or fight.

"Astral lullabies"

different world
different feeling
your heart
was my home
away from earth
into the light
your warmth
was my love
universe got me
dazed and confused
earth is lonely
many houses
but no home
many feelings
all lost
one wish
bring you back.

"Couldn't learn from icarus"

sometimes,
it doesn't feel right,
trying to fight
feelings in my heart
with all my might.
why doesn't it feel right ?
am i wrong ?
or is it my blight ?
going through the clouds,
fantasy flight,
searching for light,
falling down.
goodbye.

"Friendly shadows"

dark room,
silent breeze,
cold air,
shivers my heart.
light moves,
life moves,
window pane,
friendly shadows,
full of love.
wonder on,
wander on.

"Dead inside"

why did you go ?
where did you go ?
can't touch you,
can't see you,
lost and all alone.
kept walking,
endless roads,
searching for you.
what do i do ?
where do i go ?
i'm sorry.
thoughts of ending,
feels like bliss,
open the heavenly doors for me,

i will be there soon.
miss my friends,
miss my life,
been alone for some time.
loneliness etched in my skin,
should have fought for you,
should have chased you,
should have loved you.
now you're never to be found,
never to be seen.
where did you go ?
where did you go ?
help me,
i am dying.

"Blood flow within"

stop waiting by the river,
let your soul flow,
as the river flows towards the ocean.
just like the river,
never stops flowing,
till it finds the ocean and becomes one.
you mustn't stop,
till you find peace within.
stop waiting by the river,
and let yourself flow.

"Prison break"

prison life,
dreaming yet to awaken.
reality ? a construct of the mind,
duality defines our kind.
fools thrive,
intellects survive,
escape the escapade
into the scenic landscape.
does it end,
or does it begin ?
buffering time,
suffering mind,
rainy day,
rainy eyes,
it's not fine,
life's unkind,
time to unwind.

soulless,
soul lost,
manipulation,
self-deception,
a well of abyss,
no rock bottom,
shattered amethyst,
no glue gun.
life was once fun,
now i'm done.

"Catch me if you can"

feeling the wind,
basking in the sun,
feeling alright.
gliding through the breeze
on these two wheels,
speeding as fast as i can.
these roads,
without destination,
an endless run,
running from my past.
catch me if you can.

"Surge of chemical"

electricity in the veins,
charging up the body.
surge of infinite power within.
feel your cells,
unite them.
resistance is weak,
let it flow.
become one with body and mind,
for those who feel lost,
you are everywhere.

"Day dreaming about being a corpse

sweet kiss of death, grant me,
i'm ready,
for this life feels worthless.
i keep moving, but where am i going ?
what am i fighting ? what am i doing ?
so alone, so isolated,
watching everyone growing, alone.
a prisoner of my mind,
i can't bring her back, where do i go ?
i love you, take me with you.

"See ya later, alligator"

waiting for the message,
by the phone which never came.
winter came, summer came,
friends came, friends left.
autumn came, the wind blew,
birds chirped, the season changed.
the message never came.
goodbye, without goodbye,
nothing can be done, the moment's gone.
looking up, i see you, i feel you,
miss your touch, miss your love.
rest in peace, carry on.

"Statue"

deafening silence,
blinding lights,
breezy mood,
defeated.
bliss or pain,
no difference,
all the same.

"I get it, I'm the coolest but I'm not proud of it"

ignite my soul,
put me on fire,
i'm the sorrow,
waiting to be lit.
combustion is nature,
gasoline is the drink,
piles of bodies,
the black night.

"The show must go on"

eternal despair,
ethereal soul.
feathers everywhere i go,
yet, i don't see them.
all the advice,
i don't hear them.
are you my angel ?
i miss you.
eternal pain,
ethereal body.
blades gripping,
i feel you.
blood dripping,
i see you.
bring you back to life,
is that you ?

this journey shall go on,
as the wind blows,
sun rises,
moon shines,
trees grow,
water flows,
as nature wills,
time doesn't stop,
so make use of the minutes.

"It was never mine"

feeling of breathing,
i'm blessed.
perfection of nature,
imperfectly perfect.
it's a beautiful journey.
this life was never mine,
it was given.
walking where the wind blows,
flowing like the water in the stream,
for i am not lost,
and there is no destination.

"It's all temporary"

nothing is permanent,
all of this is temporary.
time is moving,
so are we.
don't worry if you feel sad today,
tomorrow will be better.
just hold on to tomorrow,
and let go of today.
have a good heart,
and do good deeds.
leave everything to the universe.

"Divine dialogue"

s: stolen childhood, by them.
god: by whom ?
s: i don't know.
god: all you needed was love.

"Lonely verse"

when the writer stops writing,
when the singer stops singing,
how do you come back ?
do you learn to live with it ?
when the road is endless,
no direction, no sign,
how do you get to the destination ?
when the pain is too great to bear,
when there is no one to help you,
who do you turn to ?
when you suffer,
but you understand suffering,
do you share the burden with someone,
or do you break down in tears ?
when you write this,
who do you share it with ?

"Unplanned"

floating in space,
planet of memories,
dancing and spiraling,
in their own orbit.
collision wasn't planned.
journey into the unknown,
mystery of the universe,
uncovering the secrets and truths,
of life and god.

"But was it enough?"

time slips,
moments slip,
was it enough,
did i feel ?
looking for you,
come find me,
looked into your eyes,
i see you,
i know it's you.
i am grateful,
for what i receive,
blessed.

"Once you loose you understand"

wanna hold you again,
tell you it's okay.
want to kiss you,
want to feel you.
present becomes past,
past becomes memories.
past is fading,
i am losing.
tell me you're mine,
tell me you need me,
tell me you are there for me.
remind me it's you,
tell me i found you.
lived life at the train station,
lived in fear.
fear of what may come,
it comes and goes,
painful or blissful,
like one train to another.
many trains to choose,

all different tracks,
with the same ending.
wanna spend the rest of my time,
riding the same track,
living the same moments,
over and over again.
view will be different,
but the feeling will be the same.
don't need to hold on.

"Quick change"

it's dark,
a cold tunnel,
falling endlessly,
in the abyss of emptiness.
but wait,
when the phone rings,
the spell is broken.
it kicks in-
your smile,
your eyes,
lights up my world,
like it's christmas.
and the deep abyss,
becomes the bliss.

"No time"

finding myself in the same river,
with the same feeling.
just wanna drown,
don't want to feel.
let it go,
unable to.
i am scared,
i need help.
i am on my knees,
but i got to carry on.
i wish you were here to see,
what i've become.
do you see me?
give me a sign.
no time to react,
only act.
got to keep moving.
thanks for being here for me.

"Manipulator"

manipulating the threads of fate,
ending the karmic cycle.
those who hurt me,
no wrath upon thee,
just peace.
act with love, not hate,
we are, after all, one.
must look after each other,
i keep my word and keep moving forward.
can't put down a man,
who doesn't give up.

"Let's buy the best healing out there"

let's go buy some healing,
get the best therapy out there.
let's go buy some love,
fill that void in the heart.
shop your time away,
it's time to pretend,
let capitalism win.
let's go make some more money,
work for someone else.
believe you're special,
throw away what's real,
keep looking for the best thing out there,
watch others live your life.
don't let your feelings die,
life is beautiful…
but pale light,
like white clouds with a thousand suns.
comfort me like a soft pillow.

"Here we go again"

felt your pain,
was reminded of mine.
i drowned while
pulling you out.
i guess i have to go.
it never really meant anything,
it wasn't fate,
it wasn't chance,
it was random.
maybe it will mean something in the future.
i fell in love with you like a child.
i am not hurt because i have to let you go,
i am hurt because i remembered what love felt like.
i wish you well.
life is beautiful if you open up.

"Is there any power in this stance?"

floating in oblivion,
dark violet aurora,
hovering above and around,
vitruvian man stance.
endless knots around the wrist,
spinning around,
comfortably numb in my abyss.
isolation,
is not my desolation.
this is my depth,
or what i think it is.
left myself behind,
the day you left me behind.

"6th Dimension"

it will all happen,
it will all fall.
keep holding on,
no need to push.
let it flow.
feel the wind,
weightless thought.
explore the magick,
create new realities.

"Glimpse from the past"

hazy day,
like a distant dream.
felt the fire within,
short-lived.
close my eyes,
see glimpses of us.
counting days,
to hold you again.
don't wanna rush,
can't hold on either.

"Suffering once again with better surfboard"

magnetic attraction,
a flawless connection,
gliding through the sky
like the wind.
exploring unknown worlds,
creating new realities,
weightless and formless,
no resistance in motion.
surfing the waves of fire,
no fear of burn.

"Buzz of love"

looking at the little screen,
connected by vibration.
feeling a world inside,
so far yet so close.
the buzz lights you up,
like a million fireflies,
flying up and down.
oh, how i wonder,
wander with my mind,
in my thoughts,
looking for you.
think about what we could achieve,
creating infinite realities,
feeling as one,
exploring a world full of light and colors.

bliss is this feeling,
held by fear,
what to lose,
time is still.
as long as we got each other,
till then i'll wait,
for my buzz on the little screen.

"Kiss from the past"

your soul, my body,
our worlds collide.
in the past,
ricochet into the unknown.
spinning, and spinning, and spinning,
going through a journey,
like a desert in the rain,
to find each other again.
your body, my soul,
opened what was closed.
thought there was darkness,
found love and light in my heart.
you run in my mind like the wind,
going through my lungs.
freedom is this feeling,
you gave me love once,
just like the wind, it's returned,
to open your heart,
fly like the wind again,
for all good things are wild and free.

"Only if i had the right words"

these words are meaningless,
they come from a place unknown.
all we see is pain and chaos,
we try, we try, we try,
eventually give up to the way of others,
losing identity and self.
for what we are beings of the universe,
we don't need the truth, just each other.
i don't know if it's evil or good, the ways of the world,
for i am not the creator, so i'm not the judge.
but when the right word strikes,
resonates at a frequency,
which vibrates your soul,
it tickles the nerves with endless electricity,
showing you the light and hope.
within, there's a world unexplored.

ahh… these words,
without any meaning,
without any purpose,
i want to pour on you,
but you're not here.
so these words,
attach to the paper,
into tiny letters,
like our souls intertwined the night we met.
we are apart by distance,
but attached with these words.
when you read it,
i hope you feel the same way i did.

"Try not to look within"

there is no feeling,
there is no truth,
just an empty void,
like a black hole,
absorbing all.
finding myself,
near the event horizon,
light bends,
presenting like a mirror.
see yourself running,
no escape from this escape,
once you come close.
when the stars die,
it tears a fabric in the universe.
what happens when the soul dies,
does it become a black hole too ?

"Pretender"

it hurts,
yes, so what?
i will keep breathing
and keep moving on.
i cried a lot,
but it's okay, it's in the past.
it doesn't matter,
the future holds my truth.
let's forget the present,
keep running forward.
yeah, you know, the pain doesn't last forever,
isn't that the truth ?
i need help,
but i'm proud to ask.
as you sow, you shall reap,
and you will heal on your own.
was it worth it ?

"Brand new belief"

reinforcing my thoughts,
with strong belief.
traveling through my body,
strengthening my blood.
assuming full control,
the air lifts me up.
i look up and i breathe,
feel the air in the body,
lifting my soul with passion,
unblocking my blockages.

"In the mind of an overthinker"

it hurts me

when you don't let me in.

it hurts me

when you don't try.

i hope i'm overthinking,

although i want to give you your time.

but my time is limited here,

hope you understand.

it's right now or never.

"Another act"

loud mind,
quiet heart,
in this reality.
friend and foes,
family and love,
all perception,
right and wrong.
i reside on the tightrope,
maintaining the balance,
watching and thriving,
ready to tip over.
light and dark,
don't tempt me.
i will love with passion,
but when it gets dark,
i'll move away in silence.

"No more hurt"

it doesn't hurt anymore,
it doesn't bother me anymore.
does it mean it is gone?
is this the end of the tunnel?
held onto it for so long,
coming to the light,
i will cherish.

"Bandaid on invisible wound"

are we all

a broken vase,

shattered into tiny pieces,

scattered all over,

one of a kind.

collecting them,

one by one,

over time,

bringing them together.

although some pieces are beyond repair,

some pieces are lost,

still, we,

piece by piece,

place them together,

carefully glue them.

it takes an eternity,
but we still do it.
voila, and it's finally done,
imperfect in front of others,
perfect to you.
your words,
patched my soul,
like a bandaid on a wound.
eternally grateful,
for the love i've received.

"Lovey nights"

we stayed up all night,
listening to each other's silence,
in our own bed,
breathing.

"Runner's heaven"

there is no feeling,
there is no truth,
just an empty void,
like a black hole,
absorbing all.
finding myself,
near the event horizon,
light bends,
presenting like a mirror.
see yourself running,
no escape from this escape,
once you come close.

"Dreamers plight"

wish you were here,
enjoying this walk with me.
wish you were here,
looking at the stream flowing.
wish you were here,
stuck in this dream with me.

"Coincidence at its finest"

is it coincidence,
or is it fate ?
either one,
i'm glad to be here.
separated by distance,
connected by silence,
the words you speak in your sleep,
comfort me,
knowing you slept well,
and you're alright.
with this ever-growing nature,
i hope you remain the same.
i hope you keep loving,
i hope you trust the world again.
thank you for giving me what i needed.

"Ghosts are real, they live in our head"

the pain felt so great,
i forget it all like amnesia.
but every time i come close to feel anything,
it all comes back in bits and pieces.
i collect myself,
and suddenly, i feel hopeless and helpless,
burdened by the guilt.
oh, how i miss you.
now here i am again,
redoing what was undone,
i'm walking forward,
and everyone is doing their part,
comforting me with their words.
if you could walk with me and trust me,
i could show you a different world.
sadly, it's not my decision to make,
and whatever happens,
i'll continue my walk.

"Grief : a lifetime of therapy"

when i think about you,
i lose all my words.
how can life be so cruel?
how can you leave so early?
tell me, how does it look from above?
i sense you everywhere.
what was a break,
became grief.
what was i supposed to learn?
i lost my fire,
when i lost you.
now i'm forever shuffling,
between our years,
with glimpses of us.
you made me who i am today,
i carried your torch.
the way you cared for me,
i kept searching everywhere.
i felt you in other people,
but it's not the same.

if i think more,
my tears would flow,
just like the stream in front of me,
and the fever would grip me again,
leave me paralyzed.
for the first time,
i am giving up in my life,
and i've nothing to seek for further.

"The wandering blue car"

do you remember our blue car?

we traveled to places in it.

you held my head,

we played our favorite song.

in the field,

there were calves in joy.

we were slashing water on each other.

i got grumpy,

i didn't like to get wet.

we got on the round boat,

it took us through the waterfall.

were those days even real?

i'm sorry i got grumpy at you,

you truly looked happy then.

it's been three years since you left us.

i look up, and i wonder if you are still with us.

wished you gave a sign.

i look everywhere for you,

i see you in everyone.

my soul aches in pain,

i don't question god for why you left.
my eyes are still filled with tears,
but now i've learned to hide it better.
i tried my best to replace you,
forgive me for that.
i'm still learning.
give me a sign if you are still with us.

"Hope you're looking at me"

i buried all my words,
buried my world with you.
what i was seeking outside,
was within.
do you remember the night,
we felt the breeze on our skin ?
saw the stars, camped on our terrace,
saw shooting stars.
i wonder what you wished for,
whatever you did, i've made it.
you prayed for me,
you gave me love.
do you remember ?
oh, silly me,
dead people don't remember.
if you are a ghost,
i feel you everywhere.
it's selfish of me to keep you here,
but i try to let you go.
maybe I'll try harder this time.

"Doppelganger"

i met someone today,
she reminded me of you.
she looked like you,
that's what people said.
i was too stunned to notice,
lost in my mind.
prayed to god for closure,
the other day.
and then i met her,
gave my precious love to her,
thinking it was you.
what i did to you,
she went through that.
if i could heal her,
i'll find some peace.
but feeling her pain,
left me physically damaged.

it's you who is in my mind,
but i seek you in the real world.
i wanted us to be together forever,
not like this.
maybe if i close my eyes,
rest my head on the ground,
i can see you again.

"Do you remember the "castle in the sky" music box which i brought you from china?"

i can't believe the day is here,
you are gonna leave today.
blaze of dragonfly over us,
we are dancing on our terrace.
you cried the whole night,
i believed i'd see you again.
i drove you to the airport,
how naive i was.
if i just held you tight,
and threw away your ticket,
never let you go,
things would be different.
you would still be alive.
now, like a bad dream,
unable to wake up,
i am living this life,

finding solace in material,
not my nature.
forced belief on me,
my body is angry at me,
for i harmed it.
this world has become my prison,
with no parole.
i just pray it all makes sense one day.

"Nobody wants to stay"

people said, "move on,"
i tried that.
people said, "focus on your life,"
i did that.
people gave advice,
i followed them all.
yet, i didn't realize,
people come and go,
my heart was still bleeding.
many put on a bandaid and left,
no one stayed,
i just wished someone had stayed.
now, i just want to purge,
when i think about it,
and expel it from me,
forget it like a bad dream.

waking up to each other,
and shower you with a thousand kisses,
every morning when the sun,
soothes our skin.
eat fruit from your hands,
gazing at the sunset,
it was a beautiful dream,
i am both blessed and cursed.

"Wind spoke with me and it said slow down"

suddenly, my skin tingles,
fingers move without thought.
what's within now spills out,
everything becomes vibrant.
feeling the wind's gentle touch on my feet,
music resonates with clarity, air feels pure.
oh, how i've missed you,
it was always you.
in the next life, i'll strive to be better,
work hard towards our reunion.
one day, we shall be together again.

"Lords test or is it just another way of coping"

am i in control,
or are my emotions ?
i do not know,
for that reason,
i need to test my will.
through challenges and difficulties,
i will take the lord's name,
and embrace it.

"Live now or forever seek"

i wish that what you share with others
returns to you one day
if you need help, just ask
you're not alone
look around and feel blessed
sometimes, thoughts play tricks on you; don't give in
if you can take action, do it and let go
life is short
live in the present
breathe deeply
there's divinity in the air
love without restraint
for all good things are both wild and free

"It's a beautifull life and it's bright"

we are just lost in
predicting outcomes
creating false realities
and accepting it in our head
to protect us from harm
but if we don't try
we will never know
and another life will be wasted on thoughts
stopping us from living in the now
life is beautiful when you live it

"Seekers conclusion"

voices echo in my head,
projections of people i've met,
speaking different languages,
caught up in the words' dance.
lost in translation, seeking meaning,
suddenly, all merges into one.
we're on the same boat,
heading to the same destination.
what i sought was seeking me,
love found within, free from everything.
my prayers are with you,
if you're lost in translation,
in the realm of oblivion,
let the air guide, sun warm your skin.
you will be alright again.

"Sometimes the ugly truth can be good"

and the mirror will shatter,
all the illusions,
the ugly truth presents itself,
which you've avoided for so long.
you never asked for too much,
just wanted love,
maybe in the next life, it waits for me.

"Whoa! hidden in plain sight"

a needle in the haystack,
searching for it all along.
searched all around,
years went by,
tried everything,
almost gave up.
but one day,
it took me by surprise,
while sipping our coffee,
and gazing at intercoms.
to connect while we ride through the wind,
and in that moment,
you told "just breathe".
i sought this everywhere,
met healers, readers, and more,
yet, none could provide the key.

my soul ablaze,
body consumed by pain.
now, with the wind,
i control those flames.
they may linger,
but they are tamed.

"Selfish need of love"

you didn't break me,
i was already broken.
i loved you for my selfish reasons,
believing we could mend what the world took from us.
build a nest, a life together.
you didn't cause any pain,
i simply opened my wounds,
a attempt to make you believe in the world again.
yes, i was selfish to ask for love,
yes, i was broken.
you can't break the broken,
be honest,
it's just my dream,
it shouldn't matter to you.

"You don't need a medium, you're your medium of expression"

like a dream,
you entered my life.
our skin burnt with passion,
melting our souls,
mesmerized in awe,
too stunned to speak,
i hide my face,
lost in my thoughts,
snapshots in your camera.
i wonder,
what kept us intertwined,
what caused our worlds to collide again.
i may never know,
but here we are once more.
isn't this life a dream?

how can i predict the future,
when nothing goes as planned?
yet, i know what i feel now.
no words can express it fully,
whatever i write will never be enough,
because i feel that you are enough.

"Haha from the future"

every day is a new chapter in my world,
every day we're slowly fading,
seeking deep comfort,
yet, we keep ourselves closed.
playing all sorts of games,
only to lose in the end,
while we wait for tomorrow.
i'm crafting memories with you today,
time steadily slipping away.
while you wait for tomorrow,
i'm doing my best to make you believe,
life is now, it's the best we've got.
one day, i hope we look back together,
and laugh at these fleeting moments.

"Let's leave this pain together"

the world is not always kind,
yet, there are kindred souls,
going above and beyond,
to aid a lost wanderer.
knowing you can lose yourself with them,
i refrain from judging the world.
it instills belief in me,
that you and i can shape a better world,
a better dream.
all you have to do is jump with me,
walk through the unknown forest.
while you wait for a brighter world,
i'll find the sunshine on the other side.

"Look for more"

life in a spiral,
know only three things,
to roll with the wind,
push the iron,
or to eat.
she says, "find more,"
now i delve into my mind,
see a distant future,
like cobwebs,
made of threads.
suddenly, it strengthens,
sending electricity in all directions,
all the false bonds fail,
only the real one grows and thrives.
the possibilities of the
infinity dream come true,
and now i can finally see,
my body is methane,
and her words are the spark,
that lights my soul on fire.

"Elgin nor khill was so random"

sipping tea,
under an orange sunset,
teary eyes,
courageous wind,
tall mountain,
crescent moon smiling from above,
fluffy paws chasing crows,
elgin nor khill,
a familiar feeling.
unexpected help arrived,
in an instant,
a shift unfolded,
like finding a missing puzzle piece,
i felt heard..

"Is there tranquility in the endless rest"

if there were a knob
to adjust my soul,
tune it according to you,
longing to be loved and accepted,
has left me broken and twisted.
how many times must i fall
before i learn
i don't belong here ?
every day, there's
a constant battle within,
between right and wrong.
whose voice owns my world ?
i wonder how much is left in me.
if i could just lay my head,
leave my soul with you,
i hope you take care of me.
all i long for is a tranquil rest,
where the echoes of longing dissolve into solace.

"Missed call for an overthimker"

woke up once,
looked at my phone,
hoping for your call,
just a beautiful dream,
oh that's my wallpaper.
woke up twice,
with loud voices in my head,
wishing you'd think about me,
looked for your call,
but you're getting intoxicated somewhere,
understood i didn't cross your mind.
woke up thrice,
looked at my phone,
couldn't resist, so i called,
there was no answer,
and that was my answer.
woke up in the morning,
still waiting…

"Over – heart"

You may call me an over-thinker,

Yet, you cherish the way I delve into your small details.

But when it turns to me,

You become numb and whisper, "don't overthink."

You may call me overprotective,

For once you lose, you fear losing again.

It's hard to understand but easy to feel,

Hope that day never comes for anyone.

Everyone craves true love,

Yet, when it stands before them,

They recoil from the flame,

The flame of vulnerability,

A sublime infinite love, the dream,

Invulnerability becomes the game.

Time is the currency spent,

Not here, not there,

Is not how I want to live,

My vulnerability comes from a place,

Where all the elements of nature merge into singularity,

And hence, I'm born with my "over" nature.

"More expectations"

our worlds collided
across the vast galaxy,
bound by the pull of our gravity,
we danced through the cosmos.
spiraling around each other,
connected by wavelengths,
traveling distant miles
through the echoes of our phones.
now we soar once more,
like lost stars,
without control,
awaiting a cosmic collision.
we're right here,
yet distant,
beyond the bounds of perception.
maybe i drew too near,
maybe i asked too much,
now, i've propelled you,
far, far away.
it will be alright,
with or without my presence.
i lack the strength to fight,

hoping i made you feel something real,
is only my wish.
my sole desire was to be held,
to hear sweet words of comfort.
now an empty vessel,
for everything has flown out of me.
i hope i reminded you of who you were once,
for true courage lies in vulnerability and trusting the world anew.
though i might stumble and fall,
it shall come to pass.
just embrace your authenticity,
as stars spiral again, a cosmic ballet continues

"Did you know.. we are made of stardust"

the butterfly of change
continues to float around me,
bringing heavenly signals.
the wind speaks in colors,
guiding the flame
to where my essence truly belongs.
the water shapes me,
bestows upon me a form,
a dance to survive and thrive.
the electricity within my body
breathes life into each cell,
crafting a seamless harmony with nature.

my dna, ageless as the universe's dawn,
yet preserving the child within me,
infinitely woven with colors and light,
drifts towards the future,
while tenderly embracing the past.
this creation eludes explanation,
but if we delve deep,
you might just feel it.

"Fool's lesson"

easy to hold back, keep things inside,
living a usual life 'til feelings collide.
break down in front of those who don't see,
your true worth and what you can be.
once open, now silently scarred,
hiding behind a stoic guard.
concealing pain with a practiced art,
till confessions escape and restart.
then warmth arrives, igniting the flame,
hopeless romantic, not playing the game.
fool on the hill, seeking a change,
yet, losing the warmth would be too strange.

"Its complicated"

"i said 'i love you,'
you said 'you don't love me.'
and it should have been enough
for me to move away,
but i stick by.
wonder why,
what is it in for me?
maybe i'm causing these issues
and you already gave me everything,
but i wanted more,
and you wanted less.
you gave in to your fear,
but i held the torch.
you started to change,
and i tried to come closer.
you pushed me away.
then i asked for a kiss, and you said no.
that 'no' felt like a stab,

it reached so deep.
couldn't take that.
time not spent with you
felt like a part of me missing.
got me overthinking and fighting with you
and then the cold night came.
finally, i shivered and asked,
'what did i do wrong?'
'why does fear always win?'
'why do people always become memories?'
i'll never know the answer to these,
but now i understand you need me anymore."

"Lovesick"

all i wanted was love,
but it was the hardest to give.
bodies came easily,
but love was the hardest.
though i thought i felt it,
i was wrong.
now, i rethink my whole life,
flashbacks overwhelming.
stomach twists again,
feelings left behind catch up.
how long till i break completely?
this life isn't meant for me.
longing for love was a mistake,
i don't deserve it,
and were my acts of love even real?
there won't be resistance this time,
the world has won.
i'm the problem needing fixing,
the glitch needing troubleshoot.
i'll cave in and let the world change me,
however it wants to change me.

"Stairway to heaven"

soon i'll climb the mountain
where i'll finally be free from all this
i'll carry your love and i hope it protects me
life goes on with or without me
nobody is special
i'll stay silent
i'll stay consistent
i'll stay invisible
my curse was to feel too much
my blessing was to feel too much

Author's Note

So many words left unsaid, unspoken, feelings cycling through me over and over again. I suppressed them, transforming into someone I am not. Now, I embark on a journey of rediscovery, aiming to reclaim the essence of who I once was at birth. Closure eluded me, and I hope this memoir serves as my closure, granting me the peace I seek.

If these unspoken words resonate with you, even in a small part, let it be a reminder that "help comes to those who seek." May these pages offer solace and understanding, a shared journey toward self-discovery and healing.

Unsaid

SIDDHARTH RAJ

www.ingramcontent.com/pod-product-compliance
Lightning Source LLC
LaVergne TN
LVHW041612070526
838199LV00052B/3117